A Cotton T-Shirt

Sarah Ridley

FRANKLIN WATTS
LONDON • SYDNEY

First published in 2005 by
Franklin Watts
96 Leonard Street
London
EC2A 4XD

Franklin Watts Australia
Level 17/207 Kent Street
Sydney NSW 2000

© Franklin Watts 2005

ISBN 0 7496 6059 7
Dewey classification: 677'.21

Series editor: Sarah Peutrill
Art director: Jonathan Hair
Design: Jemima Lumley

A CIP catalogue record for this book is available from the British Library.

Printed in Malaysia

The Publisher and Author thank Gosssypium for their help with this book (www.gossypium.co.uk).

Photo credits: Bill Barksdale/AG Stock USA/Alamy: 9t. Nigel Cattlin/Holt Studios: 7tr, 26cl. Bob Daemmrich/Image Works/Topham: 6b. Geri Engberg/Image Works/Topham: 16br. Mary Evans Picture Library: 13b, 15b, 25. David Frazier/Image Works/Topham: 11t. Gossypium: front cover, back cover, 1, 3, 4, 5t, 6t, 7tl, 8, 9b, 10, 12, 13t,14, 15t, 16bl, 19b, 20, 21tl, 21bl, 22, 23t, 24, 26tl, 26bl, 26tr, 26cr, 26br, 27tl, 27cl, 27bl, 27tr, 27bt. Oldrich Karasek/Still Pictures: 18t, 27clb. Bob Krist/Corbis: 18b. Novosti/Topham: 7b. Picturepoint/Topham: 11b, 21br. UPP/Topham: 29t. Watts: 5b, 17b, 19t, 23b, 28, 31. Peter Wilson/Holt Studios: 30r. Michael S. Yamashita/Corbis: 30l.Every attempt has been made to clear copyright. Should there be any inadvertent omission please apply to the publisher for rectification.

Contents

This T-shirt is made from cotton.

The story of this T-shirt starts on small cotton-plant farms in India. Cotton plants grow fibres that are made into cotton textiles. After the cotton harvest, many people work hard to turn the cotton fibres into the T-shirt.

▶ T-shirts are made from a knitted cotton textile. Other names for textile are fabric, material and cloth.

◀ There are thousands of cotton fibres inside each cottonseed pod, or boll.

Cotton plants need plenty of warm weather and rain to grow well. So the farmers plant the seeds before the rainy season. One or two weeks later, small plants poke above the soil.

Using cows to pull equipment on a cotton farm.

WORLD COTTON PRODUCERS

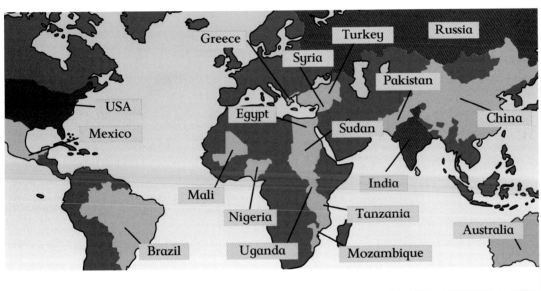

Greece
Turkey
Russia
Syria
Pakistan
USA
Egypt
China
Mexico
Sudan
India
Mali
Nigeria
Tanzania
Australia
Brazil
Uganda
Mozambique

● Main cotton producers

● Other cotton producers

Why cotton?

Cotton is a good material for making clothes. Cotton threads can be woven or knitted together to make a really strong textile. Cotton will not tear easily or wear out quickly. Because of its strength, cotton can be made into very fine, light cloth and also into thick cloth, like denim for jeans.

The farmers look after their cotton plants.

Cotton plants need a lot of water to grow well. That is why the farmers in India plant the cotton seeds before the long rainy season.

In some places, farmers grow cotton in dry areas by watering the plants a lot. This is called irrigation. They build equipment to water the plants, or even lay pipes along the fields to carry water to the roots.

▲ As the plants grow, the farmer removes weeds.

▽ This is a large, mechanised farm with huge equipment to irrigate cotton plants.

After three or four months, the cotton plants burst into flower. The flowers are white or pink, depending on the type of cotton plant.

▲ A cotton plant in flower.

When the petals drop off, the cottonseed pods, or bolls, start to develop.

◄ At first the bolls are green.

Thirsty cotton

Cotton plants are very thirsty, so cotton farmers on intensive cotton farms often use up valuable local water supplies to feed them. Sometimes this can lead to rivers and lakes drying up.

People started growing cotton around the Aral Sea in Russia about 75 years ago. It used to be a green landscape, but now it is a dry desert, dotted with abandoned boats. Cotton farming has drained all the rivers and poisoned the land.

The farmers check for pests.

While the cotton bolls are growing, the farmers look for pests. If they notice insect damage, the farmers may spray on a pesticide to kill them.

The cotton used in our T-shirt is organic. Organic cotton farmers make their own pesticide from plants and cow urine. This will kill the pests. They may also use pest traps or encourage insects that eat the pests to live on the plants.

▲ This trap attracts harmful insects away from the cotton plants.

Why farm organically?

Intensive cotton farming drains the soil of its goodness, so farmers need to use lots of chemical fertilisers. Unless used carefully, these chemicals can end up in the local water supply or food crops.

Organic cotton is grown with more skill. By growing a variety of crops, and using manure, organic farmers manage the soil without wearing it out. Organic farmers tend to have smaller farms, which means they can usually spot pests and diseases quickly before they do too much damage.

What happens on bigger farms?

When cotton is grown on huge, mechanical farms, farmers use chemicals to prevent plant diseases and kill insect pests. They could lose a lot of money if their crop is damaged. Although the chemicals used cost a lot of money, they will help the farmers to harvest much more cotton than the organic farmers.

As much as eight litres of pesticide can be sprayed on a one-acre field of cotton over the growing period.

The cottonseed pods, or bolls, split open. Now air can get in to dry the cotton fibres that are inside.

◄ The bolls split open 50 to 70 days after the plants flower.

Everyone joins in the harvest.

The cotton harvest is hard work and it takes a long time to pick all the ripe cotton bolls by hand. Heaps of cotton bolls are piled up by the side of the field.

Now workers remove the fibres from the bolls. Cotton seeds are still attached to the fibres at this stage. The cotton needs to go through a process called ginning.

Workers walk up and down the rows of plants, picking ripe cotton bolls.

Workers carry bolls to collection points.

What happens on bigger farms?

Where cotton is grown on huge farms, farmers use massive machines to harvest the cotton. First they spray the crop with a chemical to make the leaves drop off. Then the harvester strips the bolls off the plants. Inside the machine, the outsides of the bolls are removed, leaving just the cotton fibres with the seeds attached.

This photo, taken from an aeroplane, shows a cotton harvester working in a huge US cotton field.

In the past

At the beginning of the 19th century, there was a big demand for cotton. Many US landowners grew it on huge farms. All cotton at this time was

farmed and picked by hand. This was possible because the landowners owned slaves - men and women brought over from Africa against their will, who were forced to work in the cotton fields.

Huge numbers of slaves harvested the cotton crops of the USA.

The farmers sell the cotton to the ginning mill.

At the ginning mill, a machine removes twigs and dirt from the cotton. Now the cotton seeds have to be separated from the cotton fibres.

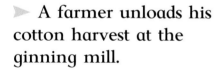
▶ A farmer unloads his cotton harvest at the ginning mill.

▲ Cotton at the ginning mill.

A machine called a cotton gin does this. The cotton is fed into the gin where the cotton fibres stick to the rough surface of a roller inside, or are caught up by saws. The machine takes the cotton fibres through a space too small for the seeds to fit, so they are pulled free of the fibres.

When the seeds have been removed the cotton fibres are light and fluffy. Machines press them into big bales, which are sold to a spinning mill.

Bales of cotton ready for a spinning mill.

In the past

Until 1793, cotton seeds had to be removed from the cotton fibres by hand. It took ages! Then Eli Whitney, from the USA, invented the cotton gin. One man turning the handle of this machine could do the work of twelve men. Later a bigger version of the machine was linked up to a power supply, allowing cotton to be ginned at an incredible speed.

One man looks after a Whitney gin as it separates the cotton seeds from the cotton fibres. Before it required many men to do this.

The cotton arrives at the spinning mill.

◄ The farmer is paid by weight, so the bales of cotton are weighed when they arrive at the spinning mill.

At the spinning mill, workers weigh the cotton and check the quality of each bale. They often mix cotton from different bales, to produce good cloth.

The mill is full of machines that do different jobs. The first machine sucks the fluffy cotton fibres up a tube to the carding machine. This machine makes the fibres line up with each other to form soft ropes.

After this, the ring-spinning machine splits up the long ropes of cotton. It takes several threads of cotton and twists them tightly together to form yarn. The yarn collects on bobbins.

◀ The ring-spinning machines turn metres of cotton fibre into yarn in minutes.

In the past

Before automatic machines were introduced, spinning wheels were used for hundreds of years to spin cotton or wool into thread. The spinner attached a bundle of cotton fibres to the spindle. Turning the wheel with one hand, she slowly pulled the bundle of cotton away from the spinning wheel. The fibres formed a long thread that the spinning wheel twisted together to produce yarn. This is still done in some parts of the world today.

A drawing from 1823. The woman on the right spins cotton fibre into a thick thread, which the other woman spins finer.

The yarn travels to the textile factory.

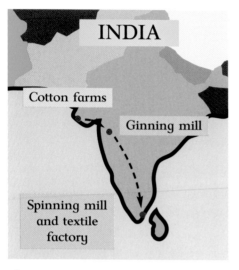

INDIA

Cotton farms

Ginning mill

Spinning mill and textile factory

▲ The cotton is taken from Gujarat in north India to south India.

At the textile factory, the yarn is made into cloth. The workers put the bobbins of yarn into the knitting machines. These machines knit the cotton yarn into cotton cloth in the same way as people knit with wool by hand, but much faster. Some machines have as many as 2,500 needles on each machine!

▲ Machine arms above the knitting machines pull cotton threads through each other to knit them together.

▼ A knitter uses knitting needles to pull loops of yarn through each other.

Knitting or weaving?

T-shirts are made from knitted cotton - loops of cotton linked together. Many other clothes are made from woven cotton. Using a frame called a loom, cotton yarn is criss-crossed over and under lengths of yarn. Look carefully at the simple cotton weaving shown here to understand how weaving is done.

Weaving thread - the blue thread goes under one red thread and then over the next, and this is repeated.

Why cotton?

Cotton is a good fabric to make into clothes as it keeps us cool. Each cotton fibre is hollow inside, which means it is easy for air to move from one side of the fibre to the other. This helps us to feel cool in cotton clothes. If we do get hot and sweaty, cotton will soak up our sweat. This also makes it great for towels and sheets.

The next stage is to dye the cotton a colour.

Before the dye is added the factory workers wash the cloth in hot, soapy water. Then they choose the dye. The dye is made from chemical powders or liquids that put colour into textiles.

◀ Powdered dyes come in every colour you can think of.

In the past

Textiles used to be dyed with natural dyes made from insects or plants. The crushed shells of the cochineal insect make a pink dye. Dye made from the roots of the madder plant turn cloth red. Different plants can be used to give other colours. These dyes are little used today because they fade quickly when washed in modern washing machines. However, some rural textile production still uses natural dyes.

The cochineal insect is specially farmed to be used to make pink dye.

Why cotton?

Without dye, all our cotton clothes would be shades of white. As most of us like to wear colourful clothes, it is great that cotton is easy to dye. Cotton cloth can also be dyed in different ways. This T-shirt has been tie-dyed. Small areas of the shirt were tied up tightly with rubber bands or string so that the dye couldn't get into them. When dry, the bands were taken off leaving areas of cloth without colour.

Workers fill a large container with water and mix in the dye. They put in the cloth and stir it around. A chemical is added to fix the dye so that it doesn't wash out when the clothes are cleaned. Finally, the cloth is dried in huge drying machines.

The cotton is dyed pink in the coloured water and pulled out onto rollers.

Workers cut out and stitch the T-shirt.

The workers lay the cotton out on work benches. Some pieces of the T-shirt are cut out by hand, others by a cutting machine.

◀ A machine controlled by a computer cuts out the correct size pieces of cloth.

Each part of the T-shirt is made by a different person who works on their own sewing machine.

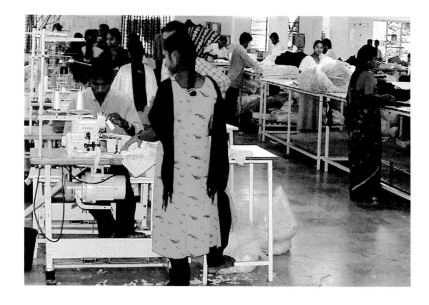

▶ Between 300 and 400 people work in this factory.

The workers use the machines to sew the front to the back, add in the sleeves and fix the neck. Now the T-shirt is ready to be finished off.

▲ Each T-shirt is checked.

▲ It took two metres of soil to grow the cotton used to make this T-shirt. Now it is nearly finished.

In the past

During the 18th and 19th centuries, many children worked in cotton mills, making cotton textiles. Mill owners paid children much less per week than adults. Small children had to crawl under working machines to mend them or to clean up. Accidents happened and some children died as a result. Many others fell ill because they had to breathe in air that was full of cotton fluff and chemicals.

Many children spent most of their day working in the cotton mills, but during the 19th century child labour was gradually abolished in the UK.

A design is printed on the T-shirt.

◄ This blue T-shirt has been stretched tightly on the machine, ready for a screen to be brought down on to it.

The printing is done by a process called screen-printing. The T-shirt is held firmly in place on a machine. Above the T-shirt is a screen - a frame with material stretched across it and the picture marked out. This is brought down onto the T-shirt and colour dye is pressed through small holes in the screen, according to the picture. If another colour is needed to complete the picture, a different screen is brought down and the process is repeated.

In the same workshop, machines print many designs.

Another machine sews labels inside the T-shirt. These say how to wash the T-shirt, where it was made and for which manufacturer.

◀ Which T-shirt would you like to wear?

Why cotton?

The same piece of cotton textile can be made to look quite different by using different printing methods or by adding embroidery. Some people use wood blocks to make repeating patterns on textiles. Others use rollers to print the same picture over and over again. Using coloured embroidery threads, pictures can be made by sewing different areas of colour onto the textile.

This colourful cotton bag is decorated with embroidery.

This cotton bag has a printed pattern.

The T-shirt arrives at the shop.

Shop workers iron the T-shirt and hang it alongside other clothes.

People look around the shop. They try on the T-shirt and other clothes. Maybe they will buy the T-shirt today.

Some people look at photos of the T-shirt in catalogues, or on their computer, and buy it that way.

Maybe the T-shirt will be right for this customer's child.

Meanwhile, the shop owners plan new designs, how many to order, where to buy their cotton and where to have their clothes made. They believe that the clothes they sell should be made from organic cotton, and from cotton where the farmer has been paid a fair price for his crop.

In the past

Before cotton was available in Europe, people wore clothes made from wool, linen or silk, depending on how rich they were. Poorer people owned few clothes because clothes were expensive. Often their clothes smelled, as it was difficult to wash and dry woollen clothes. By Victorian times, cotton cloth was cheap enough for most people to own more than one set of clothes. Cotton changed people's lives.

Three women washing clothes in the 19th century.

Follow it through

1. Farmers plant cotton seeds and look after the growing plants.

4. Everyone joins in the harvest.

2. The cotton plants burst into flower.

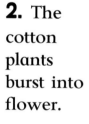

5. Workers carry the cotton to collection points.

3. The seed pods, or bolls, split open.

6. The cotton is taken to a ginning mill, where the cotton seeds are removed.

7. The cotton is taken to a spinning mill. A ring-spinning machine makes the cotton fibres into yarn.

11. The T-shirt is printed with a design.

8. At the textile factory a knitting machine makes cotton cloth.

9. The cotton cloth is dyed with a colour.

10. Workers cut and stitch the cotton cloth to make a T-shirt.

12. The T-shirt arrives in the shop and is sold.

More about cotton

We all know that cotton is used to make our clothes, but it has lots of other uses too.

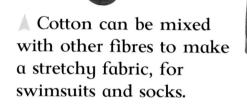
△ Cotton can be mixed with other fibres to make a stretchy fabric, for swimsuits and socks.

◁ Cotton can be made into towels. Look carefully at your towel and spot the loops of cotton.

△ Cotton is used to make bandages. It can be washed in really hot water to kill germs.

▷ Cotton is used all over our homes to make curtains, cushion covers and sheets. It washes well and lasts a long time.

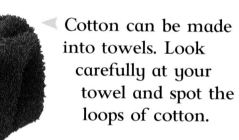

◁ Cotton can be made into tough canvas for shoes.

Look around to see how many different pieces of cotton you can see.

Recycling cotton

Cotton is made from plants so it will eventually rot away. However, rather than putting unwanted clothes in the bin, give them to a charity shop or to someone you know who will use them. Even if cotton clothes get holes in them, put them in textile recycling banks, or leave them out for doorstep

collections. There are special factories where they cut up old clothes or extract the cotton yarns from them for reuse.

The cotton plant produces two crops, not just one. The second crop is the cotton seeds which can be used to make:
- cooking oil
- animal feed
- photographic film
- soap
- fertiliser for gardens
- seeds for next year's cotton crop.

Other textiles

Plant fibres

Other plants can be used to make textiles.
The main ones are linen and hemp.

Linen is made from the stem of the flax plant. Linen is comfortable to wear but creases more easily than cotton.

Hemp is a plant that can be made into a textile. The great thing about hemp plants is that they grow well in many different countries. They are not attacked by disease and pests in the same way as cotton.

Animal fibres

Some textiles are made from animal fibres, like wool and silk.

◀ Silk comes from a caterpillar cocoon – the case a caterpillar spins around itself before it goes through the change to a moth. Silk makes a beautiful shiny fabric – soft, strong, and lightweight. It also keeps you cool.

▲ Wool can be collected from the coats of sheep, goats, rabbits and even camels! Once it is clean, it can be spun into thread and knitted or woven to make clothes. It keeps you very warm.

Manufactured fibres

Many textiles today are made from manufactured fibres. These are mostly created from coal, oil or wood.

▶ Polyester is often used instead of cotton, or mixed with cotton, because it is cheap. Acrylic often replaces wool. Nylon stretches well so it is great for tights and other stretchy clothes.

Word bank

Bobbin A reel for holding thread.

Cotton boll (seed pod) The whole seed pod of the cotton plant, including the outer case and the fibres and seeds.

Cotton fibre The thin hair-like thread produced by the cotton plant.

Cotton seed The small black seed attached to the cotton fibres.

Embroidery A form of sewing used to decorate clothes or other items.

Fertiliser A product added to the soil to improve the amount of goodness in it.

Intensive farming A type of farming where as many crops as possible are grown on the land, or as many animals as possible are reared for sale. This type of farming tends to rely on chemical fertilisers and pesticides.

Irrigation The process of watering crops using ditches, channels or equipment.

Manure Any material, but particularly animal waste, that is added to the soil to make it more fertile.

Organic A form of farming where no chemical fertilisers or pesticides are used. Organic farmers work closely with their land, using crop rotation and natural fertilisers and pesticides.

Pesticide A substance that will kill pests.

Slavery The situation where rich people own other people, slaves, who have often been taken against their will.

Textile Textiles are made from fibres. Other words for textile are fabric, cloth and material.

Yarn The twisted fibres of cotton, wool or other materials used to make fabric.

Index